ZOO
PHOTOGRAPHY

The Complete Guide to 35mm

ZOO
PHOTOGRAPHY

Text and photography
Christopher Clark

Foreword
Dr. Wayne Lynch

HUNT PUBLISHING

Hunt Publishing and Christopher Clark wish to thank the Metropolitan Toronto Zoo for
the release of the following photographs: Hippopotamus (page 13), meerkat (page 14),
Victoria crowned pigeon (page 32), cougars (page 34), scimitar-horned oryx (page 40),
African elephant (page 50), blue and yellow macaw (page 53), North Chinese leopard
(page 56), Masai giraffe (page 59), brown pelican (page 68), and white rhinoceros
(page 75).

Canadian Cataloguing in Publication Data

Clark, Christopher, 1956-
        The complete guide to 35mm zoo photography

ISBN 0-88925-622-5

1. Photography of animals. 2. Zoos. I. Title.
TR727.C592 1985   778.9'32   C85-091555-4

Hunt Publishing
1421 2A Street North West,
Calgary, Alberta, Canada
T2M 2X5

First Printing, 1985
90 89 88 87 86 85 10 9 8 7 6 5 4 3 2 1

Design: Giraffics Design Studio
Typesetting: Century Press
Separations and Printing: Friesen Printers

Printed and bound in Canada

To my grandfather,
the pleasure and inspiration
your photographs provided
will remain with me forever.

Acknowledgements

I do not think I really realized the amount of energy it would take to write this book. But, energy was the one thing I never seemed to be short of. I can only attribute this to the support and assistance given to me by the people I am about to mention. Although these people were a tremendous help during the writing of this book, it will always be their friendship I value most of all.

The thought of writing a book on zoo photography had entered my mind on several occasions, however, it was not until a talk with Bill Roth one day that I was actually motivated enough to put pen to paper.

My special thanks to Dr. Wayne Lynch, a professional wildlife photographer (and writer) who is an artist with a camera. It was his continual encouragement and belief in me that removed any doubt I may have had about my ability to write this book. In addition, the time, guidance and expert advice Wayne provided were all greatly appreciated.

I am grateful to Russ Crooks, whose background as a publications editor made him well qualified to edit this book. It was his professional approach and attention to detail that helped to convert my rough manuscripts into a form that would be enjoyable and easy to read. It was a job that came with many unreasonable requests, but one that Russ performed graciously.

The enthusiasm Elin Kelsey shared with me was never ending and always welcome. Elin's talents as a writer and zoologist, plus being a novice zoo photographer (at the time) made for a unique combination that allowed her to assist me with all aspects of this book.

To Brian Keating and Aubrey Lang for their valuable input during the early stages and their continual support throughout this project.

To Don Casson for his always enlightening conversation and as a travel companion.

To Grace Blauel, for proofreading the final manuscript.

Finally, to my wife, Lori, who has given so much of herself and asked for so little in return. She holds a special place in my life.

Contents

Cover Photograph

The vivid combination of complementary colours in this Temminck's tragopan makes it easy to see why this bird is a favourite among zoo visitors. It was photographed at a distance of 0.30 metres (one foot) with my macro lens touching the mesh of the enclosure. The exposure was f/3.5 at 1/15 of a second under overcast light.

Foreword

I have photographed wildlife for over 15 years and it has always been exciting and rewarding. I once had the opportunity to watch a pack of timber wolves interact. As the hours passed, I saw them display indifference, threats and intimidation, submission and avoidance, and this rich fabric of behaviour affected my photography and imbued it with greater depth and perceptiveness. At other times in my career I have seen elusive Malayan sun bears court and mate, a beaver nurse its kits, and a gigantic reticulated python ingest its prey. But none of these sightings occurred in the wilds of rain forests or tundra, but within the confines of modern zoos. Zoos not only provide the photographer with wildlife subjects from the common to the exotic, but some animals, such as Pere David's deer and Przewalski's wild horse, can be seen nowhere else.

Pick up any book on nature and wildlife photography and you will likely find a short section discussing zoo photography. Unfortunately, however, most of the authors hold the view that, while zoos provide excellent opportunities to practise photographic techniques, all the great wildlife photographs are taken in the wild. I disagree. Great photography, as is clearly illustrated in *The Complete Guide to 35mm Zoo Photography*, is *not* dependent upon a specific location for its greatness. A great photograph, with its qualities of originality, strong composition, and technical excellence, can be made anywhere, and certainly in zoos.

Every year, in Canada and the United States, over one hundred million people visit zoos and aquariums. A great number of these people like to take photographs, and a practical guide to zoo photography is long overdue. *The Complete Guide to 35mm Zoo Photography* fills this need. The guide is clear, concise and comprehensive. The author, Christopher Clark, brings a strong sense of order to the text, and his superb photographs not only illustrate technical principles but establish him as an expert in his field. You will find, as I did, that *The Complete Guide to 35mm Zoo Photography* is filled with helpful tips to ensure success. A must for your next zoofari.

Dr. Wayne Lynch

Introduction

A tiger turns, looks at you and growls. A killer whale does a beautiful dolphin leap. A llama nibbles on a child's shirt collar. A tropical flower blooms in the midst of winter. All these zoo experiences can be captured on film. The only limitation is your eyes and what they see. Training your eyes to see is the zoo photographer's most valuable asset. The camera is only a tool. This book will show you how to develop this skill and then utilize it to produce powerful zoo photographs.

The photography of zoo animals means different things to different people. There are those who simply want to record on film an animal they see. Their concern for whether or not the bars of the enclosure are apparent is secondary. Another way, and the one I find most challenging, is to try and eliminate any objects that may indicate the animal is captive in order to produce a natural looking photograph. By using this method, I find you are better able to enjoy the beauty of the animal.

I use the term 'natural' throughout this book to describe a style of zoo photography. What I mean by this is, that the photograph gives the animal the appearance of being wild or in its natural habitat. Some would argue that a zoo photograph cannot be natural. To me, everytime I eliminate the bars of an enclosure, I have created a more natural looking photograph. To what degree the photograph is truly natural in appearance will depend on the enclosure itself. Zoos cannot always duplicate all of an animal's natural surroundings. Compromises have to be made. Scientifically, therefore, your photograph may not be accurate. For the majority of people, this is not a problem because their photographs are only for personal enjoyment. If you are mixing zoo photographs with those taken in the wild, it is best to use the ones taken at a zoo as your close-ups of the animal. When vegetation is readily identifiable, make sure it is common to the animal's natural habitat.

Where should the new zoo photographer begin? A good place to start is with your favourite animals, whether they are the monkeys, birds, bears or cats. It is much easier to take good photographs of something you find interesting. When I first started to photograph at zoos, the only animals I photographed for months were tigers and wolves because they fascinated me. When this fascination is combined with time and patience, your photographs will reflect a new sensitivity.

Time and patience are the key words in producing photographs such as the ones that appear in this book. Therefore, visit the zoo at times when you can be alone to pursue your photographic interests. Being alone allows you to work at your own pace and concentrate on your photography.

The successful zoo photographer must learn to spend time with each animal. Walking up to one enclosure, taking a

Even though the bars of this Siberian tiger's enclosure were 1.5 metres (five feet) away from the lens, a natural looking photograph was still possible.

photograph or two then moving on to the next enclosure and doing the same thing will lead to many missed opportunities and generally less successful photographs. When I photograph an animal, I may spend many hours at its enclosure depending on whether or not I am after a specific photograph. Often, you will notice that other zoo visitors become interested in what you are doing. I find most people come over to talk to me when

To obtain termites a pygmy chimpanzee inserts a stick into the holes of termite mounds and eats the ones that attach themselves to the stick. The incorporation of an artificial termite mound into this habitat enclosure encourages this fascinating natural behaviour.

The eye of the zoo photographer should always be watching for elements of design to enhance photographs. The pattern of these three flamingos, formed by the repetition of their posture, creates a visually interesting photograph.

I am all set up; camera on tripod, cable release in hand and my lens pointed at a sleeping animal. They say, "You could be waiting all day," or "You must have a lot of patience." Sometimes they ask, "Waiting for that perfect shot?" I usually reply, "No, I'd be happy if it would just wake up."

The hardest part about being patient is knowing when to accept defeat to an uncooperative animal. The minute you have packed up your gear and turned your back on the animal, invariably, it will wake up or do something never captured on film. I have learned not to look over my shoulder. Do not give up though, as a zoo photographer who exercises patience, you will get the photographs other people miss!

Zoo photography also requires planning. Before I go to the zoo, I decide what animals I would like to photograph that day. I try to concentrate on those animals, otherwise, I find myself wandering around too much. You must be flexible though: Judge each situation accordingly and take advantage of every opportunity that interests you. If the animal you had planned to photograph is not out, do not be discouraged. Animals have a need for privacy and should not be expected to be on display all day long. Go to another animal and come back later, if time permits. When an animal I want to photograph is sleeping outside, I usually set up and wait. I find most animals, but especially birds, are still quite alert and easily distracted out of their sleep. The more visits you make to

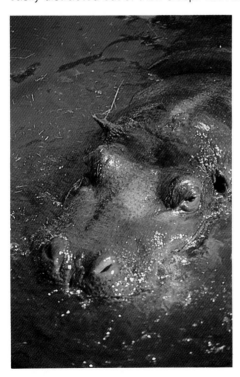

Waiting for a hippopotamus to surface requires, at most, five minutes of patience. Prior knowledge of an animal's behaviour allows you to better judge the time involved in taking a particular photograph.

Being inside does not mean you have to use your flash. This meerkat was photographed using only available light from skylights. The result is more pleasing than would have been achieved with a flash.

the zoo, the greater your chances are of obtaining the photographic results you wish to achieve.

Planning ahead not only means deciding what animals you want to photograph, but also how you would like to photograph them. My mind is full of photographs that only I can see. The challenge is to transfer them onto film.

Just as the nature photographer has an obligation not to disturb the plant or animal life being photographed, the zoo photographer should feel a certain responsibility to the animals at a zoo. No photograph is worth taking if it means you stress or disturb an animal to the point where it could injure itself. Be aware of an animal's reaction to your presence. Some animals seem to enjoy the attention they receive from zoo visitors, some will totally ignore you while others will try to hide. It is the latter that requires care on your part as all animals do not adjust easily to a zoo environment. Do not be too persistent when trying to take a photograph. If an animal seems upset by your presence, leave and try again later. In some cases, you may never be able to photograph certain animals.

Under no circumstances should you feed an animal in order to position it for a better photograph. Additional food from zoo visitors not only upsets the animal's natural diet but, alien germs contained in our food could seriously jeopardize the health of the animal or even prove fatal. If you see someone else feeding an animal, do not hesitate to ask them to stop.

Lighting plays an important part in the outcome of your photographs. This red-legged serima was photographed against a dark background to further emphasize the beautiful outline created by the use of backlighting.

Animals involved in some kind of activity, such as these two grizzly bears playing, will add interest and appeal to your zoo photographs.

Shouting at the animals or banging on the enclosures to get their attention should be avoided. So many zoo visitors do this, that the animals generally ignore it. If you want an animal to look at the camera, be creative. An animal will usually respond to an unfamiliar sound. The sounds do not have to be loud; animals with a keen sense of hearing will detect soft sounds. The sound made by slightly depressing my cable release a few times was enough to spark the curiousity of a lynx. Other sounds I have found effective are crumbling a piece of paper, rustling leaves, tapping the side of my tripod, and releasing air from a can of compressed air. These new sounds will also be ignored after you have made them a few times, so keep looking for different objects with which to make sounds.

Fences and other barriers around an enclosure are there for a reason. Certain zoo barriers can easily be crossed if one wishes. Resist the temptation. You not only risk your own safety

Nighttime animals, such as this senega galago, can introduce you to the fascinating world of nocturnal zoo photography.

Do not put your camera away just because you are at an aquarium. If you do, you will miss wonderful photographic opportunities.

but the safety of the animal as well. You can however, place your tripod on the other side of the fence. As shown by the photographs in this book, good results can still be achieved when you follow these rules.

This book has been designed to assist the photographer who uses a 35mm Single Lens Reflex (SLR) camera. However, anyone who enjoys taking photographs at the zoo can benefit by reading it. Although the majority of this book is devoted to the problems and solutions involved in the photography of animals, chapters on plants and people are also included. These two less explored areas of zoo photography can provide you with many additional hours of enjoyment.

Extinction and endangered animals are also discussed because I feel they are topics of great concern that more people should be aware of and understand. As a zoo photographer, you will become increasingly aware of the endangered aspect because more and more of the animals you photograph will be classified as endangered.

Zoo photography is challenging and exciting, the subject matter unpredictable and the results astonishing. *The Complete Guide to 35mm Zoo Photography* is meant to be the starting point and the photographs the inspiration. How far you go depends on your own interests. In any case, this book will increase your visual awareness to the photographic possibilities that await your discovery at the zoo.

Equipment

The 35mm SLR camera is the most popular format used by nature and zoo photographers. The 35mm SLR system has many merits. It is versatile and allows the photographer to select a wide range of lenses; it produces excellent quality photographs; it is compact and portable and it is reasonably priced. Most important for zoo photography is the ability to change lenses. This feature allows the zoo photographer to use longer lenses, not only to bring the subject closer, but also to minimize or eliminate distracting bars or backgrounds.

The amount of equipment needed will vary with each photographer. To ensure you do not become over-loaded too quickly remember to purchase only one piece of equipment at a time and not until you feel a real need for a specific piece of equipment.

Lenses

For zoo photography, I would suggest a telephoto or zoom lens with a focal length of at least 200mm. Telephoto lenses have a fixed focal length. They can range in size from 105 to 1200mm and they possess superb optical quality. Zoom lenses differ in that they have a variable focal length, a feature that contributes to their popularity. One zoom lens covers the range of four or five separate lenses. Popular zooms are the 70-210 and 80-200mm. The zoom lens offers an important advantage, especially in zoo photography; it allows the photographer to include or remove as much of the background as necessary without changing the camera's position. A standard telephoto lens is much less flexible than a zoom lens and the photographer must either change the camera's position or wait for the animal to move, to accomplish the same result as the zoom lens. In the past, zoom lenses were optically inferior to telephoto lenses but, this is no longer the case and today's zoom lenses produce photographs of high quality and sharpness.

You may want to look at mirror lenses, which, as their name suggests, use two mirrors to transmit an image back and forth in the lens barrel. This produces an image of similar size to that obtained using a telephoto lens of the same focal length. The mirror lens, however, is approximately half the physical length of the telephoto lens. The advantages of mirror lenses include their compact size, their reduced weight and their lower cost. Their chief disadvantage is that they have a fixed aperture (only one f/stop number, usually f/8 or f/11). Therefore, exposure can only be controlled using the shutter speed. As well, mirror lenses suffer from a loss of contrast and a certain reduction in image quality.

Macro lenses function the same way as a standard lens with two exceptions: Macro lenses will focus in much closer on a subject without the use of additional attachments and they have a higher minimum aperture (usually f/32) which provides you with one or two more f/stops. (This increased depth of field is an important consideration in close-up photography.) Available in focal lengths of 55mm, 105mm and 200mm with a maximum reproduction of approximately one-half life size or 1:2. These lenses make an excellent alternative to the standard lenses of the same focal length. A macro feature can also be found on some of today's zoom lenses, making a macro zoom a very versatile lens. These lenses usually have a maximum reproduction of one-quarter life size or 1:4. You will find this ratio more than adequate for its application in zoo photography.

In most cases, the manufacturer of your camera body will provide the best quality lenses to accompany it. They will also be the most expensive lenses. Other companies produce lenses which are more economically priced. However, the sharpness of inexpensive lenses may diminish sooner towards the edge and they may not have as many layers of coating on the lens elements which will affect their ability to render colours accurately. An inexpensive lens may not be as well constructed; making it less durable and not as smooth to operate. You have to decide whether the difference in quality, if any, is worth the difference in price.

The Normal Lens

When attempting to photograph through an enclosure, the standard 50mm lens has limited use. However, it can be used at enclosures without bars, at enclosures where you can position yourself against the bars, and at viewing windows or aquariums. The 50mm lens can also be used in conjunction with close-up rings or extension tubes to photograph smaller animals or plants.

Short Focal Length Lenses

Lenses in the 80 to 135mm range are considered short length lenses. They are usually not of sufficient power to eliminate the bars when any distance is placed between the enclosure and camera. They can be successfully used in situations similar to those mentioned for the 50mm lens. People and candid photography provide another use for shorter length lenses as they will place a bit of distance between you and your subject.

Medium Focal Length Lenses

Medium length lenses have focal lengths from 180 to 300mm. This range of focal lengths (and longer) provide the best chance of eliminating enclosure bars in most situations. Unlike shorter length lenses, you can now be positioned away from the bars and still be able to photograph through them. The majority of the photographs in this book were taken at focal lengths in the 200mm range.

Long Focal Length Lenses

Lenses that have a focal length greater than 300mm are in the longer length category. A lens of this size will allow you to take close-up photographs of the animals. In some situations, you may find you are unable to focus on the animal because it is too close to you. This problem arises because of the minimum focusing distance of the lens and can be easily overcome with the use of extension tubes (page 24).

Focusing with Medium and Long Focal Length Lenses

When focusing with medium and long length lenses, you have probably noticed that one half of the split image circle in your viewfinder tends to go dark. This happens because the maximum aperture of these lenses is usually not large enough to permit adequate light to pass through the lens and completely light the viewfinder. It is the split image area that requires the most light and the first area of the viewing screen to be affected when there is a loss of light. This effect, in no way reflects the quality of your equipment and it happens to all cameras that have this type of viewing screen. To eliminate this effect, change the angle at which you look through the camera by slightly tilting your head or the camera body. A permanent solution to this problem is to change the camera's viewing screen. Some cameras allow you to change the screen by yourself, but most must be sent back to the manufacturer. If you do not wish to change the screen, remember that your camera's viewing screen has three areas you can use to focus: The split image in the center, the microprism surrounding the circle and the matte-fresnel glass that comprises the rest of the screen. Personally, I find it easiest to use the matte-fresnel area when using my zoom telephoto lens. However, it takes time to become accustomed to using this area. The split circle should not become a crutch. If the image looks sharp in the matte-fresnel area, it will be in the finished photograph.

Films

Black and white or colour, prints or slides, the choice is yours. We all have our personal preferences. If superior sharpness and image quality are what you are after, then a good rule-of-thumb is to photograph with the slowest speed film you can use. The speed of a film is stated by its ASA (American

Standards Association) or ISO (International Standards Organization) number which indicates how sensitive the film is to light. Higher speed films are more sensitive to light while slower speed films are less sensitive. For example; ASA 100 film needs twice as much light as ASA 200 film to be exposed under the same lighting conditions. The speed of a film also affects graininess which in turn affects sharpness. Grain refers to the size of the silver and dye particles found in a film's emulsion. Slow speed films have the smallest size particles while higher speed films contain larger particles. This property becomes more noticeable when enlargements are made.

Slow speed films (ASA 25 to 32) require the most amount of light for proper exposure. Thus slow shutter speeds or larger apertures must be used in most situations. In return, you will get extremely fine grain, superb sharpness, the widest range of tones and the greatest colour saturation available in any 35mm film. Medium speed films (ASA 64 to 125) are the most popular for all-round photography. They are fine grain films producing excellent sharpness, colour saturation and tonal contrast. They also provide more range to choose from in selecting apertures and shutter speeds. High speed films (ASA 160 to 1000) provide a greater range of shutter speeds and apertures under low light situations. You can freeze action while still maintaining your depth of field. However, since graininess is increased, there will be a sacrifice in sharpness. A reduction in tonal contrasts also occurs.

The photographs that appear in this book have been taken with Kodachrome 64 slide film. It provides a sharpness and colour saturation not possible in print film. I also like using slide film because it gives visual impact when projected and excellent quality enlargements, especially when an inter-negative is produced. If you want to obtain good photographic results, do not skimp on the amount of film you use. There are too many variables in zoo photography for you to think that by taking only one or two photographs of each animal ensures a good photograph. All you should be concerned with is getting the best possible photographs you can because that particular situation may never arise again. It is a very disappointing feeling when the photographs you hoped would turn out, do not, because of subject movement, camera movement, incorrect focusing, incorrect exposure, etc. If you stay with an animal a little longer and take a few extra photographs, you may be able to avoid much of the disappointment later. This makes the extra bit of film and effort well worth it.

Tripods

Though it is probably the most disliked piece of camera equipment, a tripod (and cable release) will help to improve the quality of your photographs. A tripod holds your camera and lens, regardless of their size, steadier than you can ever hold them. You can spend a great deal of money on quality optical equipment but it is all wasted when you take hand held photographs that are out of focus because of camera movement. A tripod can help to produce razor sharp photographs. It also gives you more time to compose your photographs. You will become more aware of what you are looking at in the viewfinder and hopefully eliminate any objects that may detract from the center of interest. A tripod allows you to be more comfortable when taking photographs. It holds your camera while you are waiting for the action to happen, rather than you holding it and becoming tired or uncomfortable. The more comfortable you are, the longer your patience will last.

One thing to look for when buying a tripod is sturdiness. Tripods that have support braces from each leg to the center post are the most stable. Tripods that have quick release locks for extending the legs are preferable and safer than screw-type locks. Also, tripods in which each leg works independently, are more adaptable to different types of terrain.

Once you own a tripod, use it as often as possible until it becomes just another piece of equipment that is always taken with you. By acquiring this habit, you will consistently produce higher quality photographs.

Filters

For the zoo photographer using daylight colour film, there are three or four filters I would recommend that you have in your camera bag. An ultraviolet (UV) or skylight (1A) filter, a polarizing filter and a couple of colour correction filters. Both an ultraviolet or skylight filter will slightly warm the colours in your photograph by reducing the blue tones. They also reduce haze. These two effects are hardly detectable and the main reason for using one of these filters is to protect the front element of your lens from dirt and scratches.

A polarizing filter is the most versatile filter you can own. It can darken the blue in the sky, reduce reflection and increase colour saturation. In zoo photography, a polarizing filter can be used most effectively to reduce distracting reflections when photographing an animal through glass or one that is in or under water.

When photographing indoors with daylight colour film, you may want to use a colour correction filter instead of a flash. These filters will balance a particular light source to your film so that colours will be rendered accurately. Fluorescent lights cause your photographs to have an overall greenish cast to them. This can be corrected by the use of a magenta (FLD) filter. Tungsten lights create a yellowish-red cast and the use of a blue (80A) filter will correct for this colour shift.

Zoo photographers who use black and white film should be more aware of the different kinds of filters because they are working in a medium that can only see colour in terms of different shades of grey. Red and green are two very distinct colours but to black and white film they appear to be almost the same shade of grey. A certain coloured filter can give emphasis to one of these shades by lightening or darkening it. The same effect does not occur when colour film is used. A colour filter will shift all of the colours in the photograph towards the filter colour. This is effective when you want to enhance a sunset with an orange filter but its application is limited in naturalistic zoo photography.

Electronic Flashes

Although an electronic flash is not essential in zoo photography, it does provide either an alternative or supplementary light source. This will increase the variety of animals you are able to photograph.

The type of flash you buy will depend on your camera and your overall flash needs. For the majority of applications in zoo photography, your flash will be on manual with the light being fired directly at your subject.

A program flash, when used on a program camera provides for worry-free flash photography. An automatic flash will control exposure over a range of distances through the use of a photo sensitive cell. Usually, this flash can also be used on manual and just like a manual flash, you must adjust your exposure for every photograph.

No matter which flash you choose, an important and sometimes overlooked feature is the recycling time; how long it takes before the flash is ready to fire again. Some flashes recycle in less than one second while others can take 15 seconds or more. It can be most frustrating to miss a good opportunity because your flash was slow in recycling.

Lens Hoods

The lens hood is an accessory you should use with all your lenses. They are made of metal or rubber and screw or clamp onto the end of your lens. A lens hood prevents unwanted light rays (ones that travel directly across the front of the lens) from entering the lens barrel. Light rays that enter from the side usually bounce from element to element inside your lens and can affect both the colour and quality of a photograph. When photographing through glass, the lens hood can help stop reflections. Best results are achieved when you place the end of the lens hood against the glass. Another benefit of a lens hood is the protection it provides for the front of your lens.

Teleconverters

An economically priced alternative to longer telephoto lenses is the teleconverter. It is a supplementary lens that is placed between the camera body and the main lens and increases the focal length of the main lens. The most popular teleconverter is a 2X converter which doubles the focal length so that a 135mm lens becomes 270mm, 200mm becomes 400mm and so on. When using a 2X converter, your lens looses two f/stops. For example, if your 200mm is an f/4 lens, it will become an f/8 lens at 400mm. This is not a big problem. Your viewfinder will appear darker but your camera's built-in light meter will compensate for the teleconverter. Therefore, no exposure adjustment should be required. A teleconverter will not yield as sharp an image as your lens without the converter. This is caused by two factors: One, the converter tends to magnify any optical faults in the main lens and two, the increased focal length magnifies any camera movement so that even the slightest movement could render your photograph out of focus. One thing I have found to help correct the latter is to use a flash unit in conjunction with my teleconverter. In doing so, I can perceive no difference in image quality than using my lens without a converter.

Extension Tubes

As their name implies, extension tubes are merely hollow metal tubes that are placed between the camera body and the main lens and extend the lens farther away from the film. By increasing this distance, you decrease the lens' minimum focusing distance which in turn allows you to move in closer, increasing the size of your subject. This does not apply to zoom lenses due to the complicated arrangement of elements within the lens. Extension tubes are lightweight and since they do not contain lens elements, they do not affect the optical quality of the main lens being used.

There are two kinds of extension tubes. They can be purchased in sets of three or four, with lengths varying from 8 to 52.5mm. With automatic cameras, automatic extension tubes allows full aperture viewing and use of your through-the-lens meter while manual extension tubes do not. Extension tubes decrease the amount of light that reaches the film. If you have manual extension tubes, you must compensate for this loss of light, two f/stops when extension equals the lens' focal length. Automatic extension tubes will compensate for you. These features make automatic extension tubes the most expensive of the two.

As mentioned, extension tubes alter a lens' minimum focusing distance. A lens cannot focus on anything that is closer to it than its minimum focusing distance. A standard 50mm lens has a minimum focusing distance of approximately 0.45 metres (1.5 feet). As the focal length of a lens increases, so does its minimum focusing distance. For example: a 400mm lens has a minimum focusing distance of approximately 4.5 metres (15 feet), 800mm - 10.5 metres (35 feet), 1200mm - 13.5 metres (45 feet). With a 2.7 metre (9 feet) minimum focusing distance on a 200mm telephoto lens, what do you do if the animal you want to photograph is only 1.8 metres (6 feet) away? You can either move the camera farther away, wait for the animal to move farther away or change to a shorter focal length lens. In each of these cases, you risk including unwanted bars, too much background and a decrease in the subject's size; all of which may change the feeling or mood you originally wanted. Placing 25mm of extension tube on a 200mm lens can reduce the minimum focusing distance to approximately 1.5 metres (5 feet).

Extension tubes are also handy in zoo photography when you are interested in close-up work of plants and flowers. They will drastically increase the image size you can obtain with a 50mm lens. A standard 50mm lens produces images approximately one-eighth life size (1:8). When an extension equal to the focal length of the lens is added (i.e. 50mm), you can produce life size images (1:1). Similarly, 25mm of extension added to a 50mm lens will produce images that are one-half life size (1:2). I used a 50mm lens as an example because the shorter the focal length of the lens, the less extension you need. A 200mm lens would require an unpractical 200mm of extension to produce a life size image.

Close-up Rings

If you are unsure whether or not close-up photography is for you, close-up rings are an economical way to find out. Close-up rings screw onto the front of your lenses like filters. They can be purchased in sets of three, each having a different power (+ 1, + 2 and + 3, or + 4). The higher the number, the closer you can get to your subject. Close-up rings can be used in combination, two at a time. Always remember to place the more powerful ring next to the main lens. Being lightweight and compact, these rings can be easily carried in your camera bag. Image quality is one disadvantage because they do not produce photographs as sharp as macro lenses or extension tubes. Using a higher aperture setting can diminish this problem. Also, close-up rings must be of the same diameter as the front of your lens, which makes them less versatile.

Auto Winders and Motor Drives

An auto winder or motor drive attaches to the bottom of the camera and automatically advances the film after each photograph. An auto winder will advance the film up to two frames per second while the motor drive can advance from three and one-half up to five frames per second. Under certain circumstances, an auto winder or motor drive will allow you to photograph a certain action or feeling that you may have missed otherwise. If you are just starting to buy accessories for your camera, I personally feel the money might be better spent on quality lenses.

Depth of Field

Once you have focused your lens on a particular subject, the depth of field is the amount of the photograph that is in sharp focus in front of and behind your subject. Three factors affect depth of field: the size of the lens opening (aperture), the focal length of your lens, and the distance between the camera and the subject. As you become more familiar with these factors, you can use depth of field as a creative tool to take better photographs.

The amount of depth of field is not equal in front and behind your subject. One-third of the depth of field occurs in front of your subject and two-thirds occurs behind.

Lens Opening

The aperture ring on your lens is marked in a series of f/stop numbers. Regardless of focal length, as these numbers increase, the size of the lens opening gets smaller and the depth of field will increase. Therefore, at f/22 you have greater depth of field than at f/16 or lower. As these numbers decrease, the lens opening gets larger and the depth of field decreases. Depth of field becomes very shallow at maximum aperture (the smallest f/stop number on your lens), and only a few inches may be all that is actually in sharp focus!

Relationship between aperture settings

← amount of light doubled with each f/stop
depth of field decreases

| f/2 | f/2.8 | f/4 | f/5.6 | f/8 | f/11 | f/16 | f/22 |

amount of light halved with each f/stop
depth of field increases →

F/stop numbers also control the amount of light that reaches the film. Everytime you adjust the lens opening one f/stop, you either cut the amount of light reaching the film in half or you double it. Moving from a small f/stop number to a larger one decreases the amount of light reaching the film, while going from a large f/stop number to a smaller one increases the amount of light.

Subject Distance

The farther your subject is from the camera, the greater the depth of field. This occurs regardless of the focal length of the lens in use. Conversely, if your subject is close to the camera, the depth of field is less.

Focal Length

The term focal length describes the distance (in millimetres) from the center of the lens to the film when the lens is set at infinity. As the focal length of the lens is increased, the depth of field will decrease. In other words, a 28mm lens set at f/5.6 will have more depth of field than a 200mm lens set at f/5.6 when they are both focused at the same distance.

Depth of Field Preview Lever or Button

If your camera is equipped with a depth of field preview lever or button and you never knew what it was for, now is a good time to learn. With the use of the previewer, you can tell if the enclosure bars are being included before you take the photograph.

Today's cameras have maximum aperture metering that allows the viewfinder to remain bright regardless of the aperture setting. When you press the shutter release button to take a photograph, the lens closes down to the actual f/stop you have selected, the mirror flips up, and shutter opens to expose the film.

When you push the depth of field previewer, you cause the lens to manually close down to the actual f/stop you have set. In the viewfinder, you obtain a visual indication of what will be in focus in the finished photograph. When the bars of an enclosure cannot be eliminated, they will appear as out-of-focus grey areas at smaller f/stop numbers. As you increase the f/stop number, the bars appear sharper.

When your lens is set on its maximum aperture and the depth of field previewer is pressed, nothing happens. The viewfinder remains bright because your lens is already wide open. Therefore, what you see in the viewfinder is exactly what will be in focus in the finished photograph.

In certain situations, such as when you are very close to or touching the enclosure with your lens or when using a long focal length lens, you may be able to use a larger f/stop with no hint of the bars appearing. By all means experiment. Make sure, however, that you use the depth of field preview to check for the bars before you take the photograph.

Exposure Problems

Have you ever looked at one of your photographs and wondered what went wrong? I am sure we have all found ourselves in this state of bewilderment from time to time. The two biggest problems faced by most photographers are out-of-focus and incorrectly exposed photographs. Incorrect exposure usually results from an unusual lighting condition which your camera's meter was unable to read properly. According to one of the leading camera manufacturers, the light meter in your camera will determine correct exposure roughly 80 percent of the time.

There are three ways to use your light meter: One is to use it unquestioningly. This means 20 percent of your photographs may not be properly exposed. Secondly, you can use it as a guide towards a final decision on an exposure, or thirdly, you can ignore it. I suggest you avoid the first, experiment with the third and perfect the second.

Using your light meter as a guide means you must know how a light meter works and when to override it. Light meters try to make everything middle or neutral grey (18 percent grey). Pure white and solid black will become neutral grey if your meter has its way. This can create such new sub-species as the 'neutral grey panther' and the 'middle grey polar bear'! The same problem arises when extremes of light and dark occur within the same photograph.

Overriding your light meter is simply a matter of adding light to, or taking light out of the photograph. Just remember, if your camera does not have an exposure override dial, you must switch your camera into the manual mode when making exposure corrections.

Let us look again at our two sub-species to see what the meter decided and how we can correct for it. We are photographing a black panther which is filling most of the frame, the meter will try to make it neutral grey by overexposing the panther in order to lighten the black to a grey. To correct this situation, underexpose the photograph by using a shutter speed one or two times faster than the meter suggests. This will put the black back into the panther. What if a polar bear is filling most of the frame? The meter will try to make the white polar bear neutral grey but, this time it will underexpose the photograph to darken the white to grey. Knowing this, we simply overexpose by using one or two shutter speeds slower than the meter suggests to put the white back into the polar bear.

The above two examples have shown what happens if the photograph is predominantly light or dark, but what happens when you have a light subject on a dark background? Exposure

Underexposed or overexposed? In this case, neither. Even though the white gyrfalcon does not balance the dark background in size, it is closer to the center of the photograph where 60 percent of the camera's meter reading is taken.

No exposure compensation was made to the photograph on the left. Underexposing the muskox by one f/stop has returned the deep rich colour to its coat.

correction will depend upon the relationship between the area the subject occupies and the area of the background. If a light subject dominates the picture area but a dark background is included, you will still overexpose for the light subject but to a lesser degree. As the dark background becomes more dominant, the light meter will be increasingly affected by it. If you find a situation where the light and dark areas seem equal when looking through the viewfinder, exposure compensation will not be necessary because both extremes will cancel each other and the light meter should expose the scene properly. When a light subject is on a predominantly dark background, the meter will again try to make the dark background a neutral grey and will overexpose the photograph. But this time your light subject will also be overexposed and become washed out. Therefore, if you want the light subject to be properly exposed with good detail and definition, you must underexpose by using one or two shutter speeds faster than the recommended setting. You can apply this rule to a dark subject on a light background simply by reversing the principle.

Large areas of light or dark can affect proper exposure of the main subject. This photograph was overexposed by one f/stop to insure the bald eagle did not become too dark.

Reciprocity Failure

Using long exposures (two seconds or more) because of slow or medium speed film, the low level of available light or the need for maximum depth of field, (most commonly found when photographing reptiles or plants without a flash), can cause what is known as reciprocity failure. It is the inability of the film's emulsion to react as quickly to low light intensities as it would under normal conditions. The result is underexposure. To correct for this problem, you must increase the exposure. For exposures between two seconds and one minute, add half the recommended shutter speed. For exposures more than one minute, you should double the recommended shutter speed.

Colour shift tends to go hand-in-hand with reciprocity failure. Films tend to be either warm or cool in their colour rendition. It is this characteristic that is exaggerated by long exposures causing your photographs to shift towards one dominant colour. Kodachrome 25 is the least affected. The effect increases with higher speed films. Colour shift is minimized by correcting for reciprocity failure, photographing under overcast conditions (which unlike direct sunlight, does not transmit any colour of its own) and using slow speed film.

Reading about exposure compensation may seem a bit confusing and in order to understand the principles in this chapter, you must apply them. When you first encounter situations that you think the meter may read incorrectly, take one photograph at the meter's recommended setting. Then, override the meter to what you think is the correct exposure. Comparing the two photographs will help to strengthen your understanding of exposure.

Enclosures

For the zoo photographer interested in creating natural looking photographs of animals, most enclosures present the same basic problem; eliminating the bars. Today, more and more zoos are solving this problem by removing the bars from one or more sides of newer habitat enclosures. Despite advancements, you will still be faced with enclosures that use bars, mesh or fencing.

Regardless of the focal length of the lens, when you are attempting to photograph through an enclosure, one of the most important factors to consider is the aperture of the lens. Using maximum aperture (the smallest f/stop number) produces a shallow depth of field which hopefully causes the bars of an enclosure to be out-of-focus. Objects that are sufficiently out-of-focus actually seem to disappear in your camera's viewfinder and in the finished photograph.

Taking photographs at maximum aperture requires precise focusing on your part. This is especially true when using longer lenses. You will be working with a minimum depth of field which leaves little room for error. The thing to remember, as with the photography of people, is that it is the eyes that are the key to a successful photograph. Even if it is only the eyes that are in sharp focus, the photograph will be both pleasing and acceptable. If you find it difficult to focus on the eyes when the animal is far away, you can focus on other parts of the animal that are on the same plane as the eyes. For example, on cats, try focusing on the whiskers.

Before maximum aperture can do its job, you must also concern yourself with two distances: The distance between the camera's lens and the enclosure bars, and the distance between the enclosure bars and the animal being photographed. The ideal situation occurs when you can position your lens against the enclosure. But, in many areas of a zoo, are lower secondary fences placed around an enclosure. When photographing at such an enclosure, you may find yourself up to 1.8 metres (six feet) from the bars. You can decrease this distance by placing your tripod on the other side of the fence. This will position your lens a little closer to the enclosure and could mean the difference between the bars being included or eliminated from the photograph. When your lens is not able to totally eliminate the bars, you may notice narrow strips in the viewfinder that appear to be out of focus or slightly lighter than the surrounding colours. This effect may be subtle enough to go unnoticed (unless one of these strips falls across the animal's eye). If you find you are having trouble getting the eye or eyes in sharp focus, this is probably the reason. Adjusting the camera position slightly will move the bar

Accurate focusing is essential when working with close-up or telephoto lenses and maximum aperture. In this portrait of a Victoria crowned pigeon, where depth of field was very shallow, it was critical that the eye was in sharp focus.

away from the eye. When you are positioned at these farther distances and the animal is positioned farther back in the enclosure, you will generally be able to eliminate the bars by using the proper focal length lens, maximum aperture and choosing the right camera position.

When faced with a variety of situations, lenses with a focal length of 200mm or longer will prove to be the most valuable in eliminating the bars of an enclosure. However, your standard 50mm lens can certainly be utilized under certain circumstances. At an enclosure housing an animal that is not particularly dangerous, it may be possible to place your lens against or right through the bars or mesh. When there is a fine wire mesh, try to center your lens between the wire as much as possible. When using a 50mm lens, you must exercise special care in your composition because much of the surrounding area will be included. Thus, it may be difficult to eliminate distracting objects that can render your photograph unacceptable. To minimize this problem, always set your lens at maximum aperture, and wait until the animal moves closer to fill more of the picture frame; leaving less room for the background.

The times when you are positioned against an enclosure are the times you should be the most alert. Even the laziest looking of animals can have lightning reflexes. It also pays to remember how many animals there are in an enclosure. I was once photographing a pair of bobcats, their enclosure had a secondary fence around it except for one area that had a row of telephone pole-sized logs. A gap between two of the logs

These two cougar photographs show how aperture controls depth of field. They were both taken with the camera 1.5 metres (five feet) away from the enclosure. For the one on the left I used f/22 and for the one on the right, f/3.5.

was large enough for me to place my lens between them, and very close to the enclosure mesh. One of the bobcats was lying directly in front of me. I became so involved in photographing this animal that I forgot about the other bobcat. It seems he took an interest in me though, because the next thing I knew he had jumped up onto the mesh. His paw came through the mesh and landed on top of my lens. Obviously startled, I looked up and there was a bobcat looking right at me!

Being farther away from an enclosure does not mean you are completely safe either. If you are ever photographing tigers and one of them turns and puts its backside to the enclosure, run, and if you can, grab your camera! Tigers, being territorial, periodically spray their enclosure with urine to leave their scent. Being the largest of all the cats, they spray quite far, and if you are less than 1.5 metres (five feet) away you could be the most pungent smelling zoo visitor around, unless of course there was another photographer standing beside you!

Camera Positioning and Shadows

Many different sizes, shapes and colours of enclosures will be placed between you and your subject. Enclosures with dark coloured bars will prove to be the easiest to photograph through because they reflect very little light. It is the reflection from lighter coloured bars that makes them the most difficult to eliminate. Even if you are able to photograph through the bars, this reflection can cause a decrease in colour saturation. Your best chance of eliminating the bars, regardless of their colour, is to position your camera so as to photograph through an area of the enclosure that is shaded. This usually reduces the reflection from lighter coloured bars enough to enable you to photograph through them. Shadows will also make it even easier to eliminate darker coloured bars. Trees, viewing bays and enclosure support posts will cast shadows over parts of an enclosure. Do not forget your body, especially your hands which work nicely when you are positioned against an enclosure.

When I speak of a shaded area, I am not implying that it must be a large area. It only needs to be large enough to allow your lens to photograph through. Even if you are positioned 1.5 to 1.8 metres (five to six feet) from the enclosure, a 200mm lens only needs a shaded area less than 30cm (one foot) in width. Obviously, the larger the shaded area, the better it will be especially if the animal is moving. Practice surveying an enclosure when you first arrive to locate all available shadows and then decide which ones will enable you to obtain the best photographic results.

The same objects that cast shadows on an enclosure, helping you to photograph through it, can also cast shadows on your subject. This can detract from the overall photograph, if they fall across the animal's face. Natural shadows such as

There is no mistaking the vertical and horizontal lines on this ferruginous hawk. They were cast by the bars of the enclosure and can be overlooked when too much attention is focused on only the subject.

those created by trees, are acceptable if they fall over the body of the animal. Shadows caused by the enclosure itself are easily recognized and should be eliminated from the photograph whenever possible. As I have learned, the obvious is sometimes the unnoticed, particularly when the animal is located in what seems to be a beautiful position. In the excitement of trying to get a nice photograph, it is possible to overlook the most obvious shadows; until of course, you get your photographs back from the lab.

When an animal is stationary and you are able to position your camera against the enclosure, place your hand between the angle of the sun and the end of your lens. The shadow cast over the bars will make photographing through them easier. You may find, as I did, that you could have used a third hand. To overcome this problem, I constructed a cardboard shade maker that is portable and hooks onto the bars of the enclosure

The long-eared owl on the right was photographed with the aid of a shade maker. The owl on the left was not. A shade maker reduces or eliminates reflection off an enclosure and increases the colour saturation in a photograph.

(page 89). This device allows my left hand to remain on the focusing ring ready to adjust for slight movements of the animal. Similarly, a piece of black broadcloth held over the lens and attached to the enclosure with clothes pins can be used to create a shadow.

Viewing Windows

Enclosures with viewing windows will allow the photographer who does not have medium or long focal length lenses to still take some good zoo photographs. No matter what lens you use, whenever photographing through these windows, be sure that your lens hood is touching the glass. In this position, the lens hood prevents reflections of yourself or whatever is behind you, from being included in your photograph and causing a loss in image quality. A polarizing filter can also be added to reduce reflection. Touching your lens hood to the glass helps to prevent any imperfections in the window such as scratches, from affecting the image. But, it is still a good idea to look for the cleanest section of the window and to use your lens on maximum aperture.

To eliminate distracting backgrounds when using a smaller focal length lens through a viewing window, shift the camera downward and include more foreground. Be careful of reflections. The bottom of your lens will be slightly away from the glass and if they occur, do not take the photograph.

Animals behind glass always give me my biggest scares because the barrier does not seem as real to me as metal bars. I have had polar bears lunge at me on several occasions which, believe me, is a real heart stopper! I sometimes wonder who decided how thick to make the glass and how it was tested.

Choosing an Enclosure

The ease of photographing through an enclosure varies with the time of day. As the sun moves across the sky, light and shadows are constantly changing; as are the photographic opportunities at a particular enclosure.

An enclosure that is perfect for photographing through in the morning may prove impossible in the afternoon. Enclosures with many sides and angles provide you with the most photographic possibilities. Having a zoo located in the area where you live, gives you an advantage over a visitor to the zoo. You can become familiar with all the enclosures to the point where you know exactly which animals you can photograph at a particular time of day to obtain the best results.

Weather
Conditions

There are no bad days on which to photograph, just different ones. Knowing what to expect on different days will enable you to take advantage of the conditions which best create the mood or feeling you want to portray.

Bright Sunshine

The majority of zoo photographs are taken on sunny days for no other reason than we enjoy being outside in this kind of weather. On such days, it will be easiest to eliminate the bars of an enclosure from your photograph due to the dark and distinct shadows that can be cast on an enclosure. But, remember sunlight can be harsh or beautiful, so choose your situations carefully (page 45).

Haze

Hazy days are good days to photograph animals as colours appear more natural. The soft light, characteristic of these days, allows middle tones of colour to be intensified as opposed to the light and dark contrasts of a bright sunny day. On a hazy day, the sun is partially hidden by thin clouds but shadows are still evident, making it possible to photograph through an enclosure.

Overcast

Overcast light does not transmit any colour of its own and there is a minimal amount of reflection. Therefore, an overcast day will enable you to reproduce an animal's colours most accurately, with the greatest amount of colour saturation. However, on overcast days, it is more difficult to photograph through enclosures with lighter coloured bars because shadows are non-existent. You will have to experiment on these days; as enclosures with darker coloured bars may still allow you to photograph through them. As an alternative on such days, try photographing at enclosures which have viewing windows or those that do not have bars.

Rain

If you are looking for a challenge, photographing animals when it is raining will certainly provide you with one. Rain tends to be a very dull visual effect, therefore, the trick is to find ways to emphasize it. Two ways are to photograph rain against a dark background or during a sun shower. This will highlight the rain and produce a stronger photograph.

Falling rain will appear streaky at just about every shutter speed, but, slower shutter speeds (below 1/30 second) will ensure the rain is highly visible and heighten the overall effect.

Most animals do not run inside and hide in the back of their enclosures during a storm. They will usually either sit it

This pleasing winter photograph of a snowy owl was accomplished by isolating the subject and the falling snow against a dark background. A shutter speed of 1/125 of a second was used.

Start to create dramatic sunlit photographs once you learn when and how to use sunlight to its best advantage.

This scimitar-horned oryx and young were photographed under hazy conditions. There are no extremes in contrast between light and dark and a greater range of middle tones are present.

out or seek shelter under a tree or rock, but generally you will still be able to photograph them. In fact, I have seen falcons and owls thoroughly enjoy the soaking they received from a good downpour.

Snow

I have sat with animals while it was snowing for three and four hours just waiting for a real blizzard to happen. Unfortunately, this is a photograph that has eluded me so far. However, the one thing I always notice is not only the lack of zoo visitors but, the complete absence of zoo photographers. I am sure there are photographers who brave the cold and snow but, they are few and far apart. For those who have not tried this exciting

Overcast light has most accurately reproduced the colours of this goshawk. Unlike sunlight, overcast light does not transmit any colour of its own.

opportunity; I find it much easier to venture out into a storm if I look at the excellent photographic possibilities rather than any discomforts I may or may not suffer.

Photographing falling snow is easier than photographing rain because the visual effect snow produces is stronger. However, you should still look for darker backgrounds to give emphasis and create a more successful photograph.

When photographing falling snow you should decide whether you want it to be sharp or blurred. To freeze falling snow, use shutter speeds of 1/125 of a second or faster depending on how heavy the snow is falling. This can create a very pleasing photograph by capturing each individual snowflake. If you want to accentuate the storm or the effects of any wind on the snowflakes, use a shutter speed of 1/15 of a second or slower. This will create the impression of motion by streaking the snowflakes. When you stop down your lens to reach these slower shutter speeds, remember that depth of field increases and depending on your camera's position, this may not be desirable when photographing through bars.

Rain or snow, you must protect your equipment from the elements. An ordinary plastic bag, large enough to cover your lens and camera will generally do fine. Cut two holes in the plastic, one for the front of your lens and another for the eyepiece. Use a lens hood to protect the front of your lens and to keep it clear. Also, check your film counter before you go outside. If you are nearing the end of the roll, you should replace it. By doing so, you will usually not have to open the back of your camera to change films once you are outside.

Seasons

Photographing at zoos that are located in more northern latitudes offer a variety of seasons and provide you with many different opportunities. Northern zoos in spring, give you the chance to photograph newly born animals with the possibility of

This curious little cougar kitten is a perfect example of why springtime at the zoo can hold many unique and enjoyable opportunities when it comes to photographing young animals.

In more northern zoos, autumn is certainly the time when you will produce some of your most striking colour photographs.

following their development throughout the summer. Also, animals that have been inside all winter may be more active once they are outside again in the spring.

Summer is an enjoyable time to be outside as proven by zoo attendance figures. However, it is not necessarily the best time to photograph animals unless you visit the zoo in the early morning or late afternoon when the lighting is not so harsh.

Fall is the most beautiful time of year with leaves changing colour and covering the ground. Animals such as deer, moose and elk will have a full rack of antlers at this time. Certainly an impressive sight.

Winter, the time when the least number of people visit northern zoos, is actually the best time to photograph predators. They will be more active than on those hot days of summer. Their fur coats will be at their thickest and most beautiful stage. Having snow on the ground can also help produce a more natural looking setting. No one would know that the enclosure floor is made of concrete once it is covered with a layer of snow.

Snow has covered the concrete floor of this polar bear's enclosure and helped to produce this natural looking photograph not possible during any other season.

Time of Day

The properties of light I describe here relate to sunny days. When photographing on hazy or overcast days, the type of light produced is softer with no definite direction and will vary slightly in intensity throughout the day. Its colour does not change, therefore photographing at any time during the day will yield similar results.

The most pleasing photographic results on sunny days are generally obtained during early morning or late afternoon when the sun is lower in the sky. At these times, light rays must travel farther through the earth's atmosphere which scatters the light and filters out the blue-green rays. The red rays reach the earth and give the sun its yellow-orange appearance. During early morning and late afternoon, these warm rays will impart the colours of your photograph with a richness and saturation that can be absolutely beautiful. The fur and feathers of animals are especially attractive in low angle light. Most of my favourite photographs have been taken using early morning or late afternoon light.

At noon, the sun is directly overhead and the light is generally harsh. Very few light rays are filtered out at this time. Reflection, which at noon is at its greatest, can cause a deterioration of image quality and a loss of colour saturation. Reflection also creates many highlights on the bars of an enclosure. This, plus the fact that shadows are shorter, usually makes noon a difficult time to photograph through enclosures.

This photograph of an orang-utan taken at noon shows how direct overhead sunlight can wash out detail and colour.

Lighting conditions not only change throughout the day but also throughout the year. The farther north of the equator you are, the greater the difference you will notice. In the summer, the sun travels high in the sky and the light is strong. Photography outside should generally be avoided between late morning and early afternoon. In winter, the sun is travelling close to the horizon, producing low angle light for most of the day and making it possible to photograph throughout the day.

Early morning light has enriched the cream and brown coloured feathers of this short-eared owl and accentuated the contrast between the warm tones of the owl and the cool tones of the dark green background.

Lighting

Lighting is a creative tool similar to composition. Where you place your subject in relation to the sun can dramatically affect the impact of a photograph. There are three basic types of lighting: Frontlighting, sidelighting and backlighting.

Frontlighting

This type of lighting occurs when the sun is positioned above and behind the camera so that sunlight falls directly on your subject. Frontlighting can create very dramatic effects, especially when it separates an animal from a darker background. Due to shadows being cast behind the subject, shading is not present on the subject to indicate dimension and your photographs may appear flat.

Sidelighting

I find sidelighting the most pleasing type of lighting for zoo photography. It occurs when the sun is positioned to the side of the camera and subject. This type of lighting helps to define the shape of, and add detail to the animal. In addition, low angle sidelighting (and frontlighting) can be used to successfully eliminate the bars of an enclosure due to the long shadows they create.

Photographing this gemsbok using frontlighting has yielded an acceptable photograph with good colour. However, with no shadows visible to define shape and volume, the photograph looks very two-dimensional.

Sidelighting produced the tremendous visual impact this addax projects. Only this type of lighting will add such detail to fur and horns. Isolating the subject against a shadowed background also strengthens the overall effect.

This black bear cub (in a cinnamon phase) looks extra round and fuzzy because sidelighting creates shadows which define shape and emphasize detail.

This early morning backlit photograph of an alpine ibex was possible because I was able to place my lens between the bars of the enclosure eliminating any strong highlights on the bars from appearing in the photograph.

Backlighting

This type of lighting is the most dramatic and occurs when the sun is placed in front of the camera and behind the subject. Backlighting is also the most difficult lighting under which to photograph. It casts highlights on the backside of the enclosure bars which are next to impossible to eliminate. Unless you are photographing at an enclosure without bars, the best course of action is to partially backlight and sidelight the animal.

Experiment with backlighting; it can create beautiful highlights on animals with fur, outlining their coat in a rim of light. Your subject might be very dark, which is acceptable. If you want more definition in your subject, you must overexpose by one or two f/stops. A word of caution; backlighting places you in a position where sunlight can directly enter the lens causing streaks of light known as lens flare to appear. This effect can either enhance or ruin a photograph. It is easily controlled by placing your hand above the camera and between the sun and the lens to shade the end of the lens.

The Eye of the Photographer

Having a good working knowledge of your equipment and an understanding about exposure does not guarantee that you will produce a successful photograph. It helps, but more important is the ability to see and be aware of what you see.

Photography is visual communication. Photographs can tell us stories, stir up emotions and show us things we have never seen. The photographs that accomplish this are taken by photographers who have an ability to see. You can take all kinds of technically perfect photographs that say nothing. The photographs we remember are the ones that need no explanation.

The problem that frequently faces most photographers is that they see something they want to photograph but somehow the finished product never quite conveys the feeling or mood that was present at the time. Invariably that feeling or mood has to be explained. The solution is to identify what made you want to take the photograph in the first place and then try to emphasize that part. Was it a colour or combination of colours, a texture, pattern or an interesting shape? These are all elements of design that you should be aware of and train your eyes to look for. As a zoo photographer, you will find these elements all around you.

Shape

The shape of an object is an element of design that can produce a strong visual impact and animals are ideal subjects. Shape is best emphasized by isolating the animal against a contrasting background. This can be accomplished by backlighting the animal or lowering your camera angle so that the background is mostly sky. In both these cases, it is the shape that is dominant, with colour being secondary. This creates a very graphic image. Another way to emphasize shape is to frontlight the animal against a contrasting background. This can best be achieved in early morning or late afternoon light because of the long shadows that fall on the background. This technique while still emphasizing shape, allows the element of colour to further increase the visual impact.

Colour

The variety and beauty of colours found in the animal world are endless. Nature has given each animal a certain set of colours for a specific reason(s); from camouflage to attracting a mate. Birds are the most strikingly coloured of the animals. They do not need the muted earthy tones of most ground dwellers because they can escape to where few can follow.

The skin of an African elephant is anything but smooth. Closing in on the subject and the use of sidelighting has emphasized this element in an effective way.

Colours in photography play an important role in creating mood and impact. Look for warm colours, such as red, orange and yellow, when you want to create a feeling of excitement or tension. Cool colours such as blue and green are most effective to evoke quiet and peaceful moods. Colour has the power to instantly draw your eye to a specific part of the photograph. The yellow eyes of a snowy owl are an excellent example. This drawing power can also work against you if the strongest colour does not happen to be part of your center of interest.

Lighting conditions can change the way in which the eye and camera perceive colours and will effect the visual impact of the photograph. For more specifics, see the chapters on Weather Conditions, Time of Day and Indoor Photography.

When you want to emphasize shape, choose animals that lend themselves to this element. Photographing this flamingo later in the afternoon when long shadows were cast in the background has isolated its beautiful curving neck and produced a strong impact.

Texture

The tactile quality of an object appeals to our senses. When your photograph conveys a texture to the point where you can almost feel it, you have created a strong photograph. Animals make excellent subjects for texture. Think of the soft thick fur of a snow leopard or the rough skin of an African elephant. Texture is best emphasized by light and shadow which means photographing under sunny or hazy conditions. Also, close-ups are the best way to accentuate an animal's texture.

This blue and yellow macaw is an excellent example of how colour can have a tremendous visual impact on the eye.

The repetition of the peacock's 'eyes' in its tail feathers has created an interesting wallpaper type pattern.

Pattern

Pattern is created through repetition. It can instill harmony and order in a photograph and is an effective element of design. A deviation in any pattern because of colour, position, or shape will disrupt the harmony, resulting in an even more dynamic photograph.

Look for pattern in the animals themselves. The stripes of a zebra or the spots of a jaguar are two examples. The most eye-catching type of pattern is the repetition of shape. However, it is also the most difficult kind of pattern to find because it is rare to have several animals in the same position right beside each other.

Now that you know some of the elements that, when emphasized, create a strong photograph, use them, along with good compositional skills and your technical knowledge to produce photographs with visual impact. This ultimately separates you from the photographer who simply takes pictures.

Composition

The elements of a successful photograph rarely just fall into place. They must be examined, simplified and organized effectively within the photograph to create a strong composition. Composition should happen in the camera's viewfinder, not in the darkroom or the photofinishing lab. By following this simple rule, you will become a better photographer because you will be forced to be more aware of what you see. Slide film can be an unforgiving teacher since the way you photograph a particular subject is exactly the way your viewers will see it. All the photographs in this book are shown exactly as I photographed them. They were purposely not cropped in order to demonstrate that composition can be done in the viewfinder and done consistently.

If you want to produce natural looking photographs, an animal's enclosure can place many restrictions on composition, making it difficult at times for you to do what you want. This factor has one advantage, it forces you to simplify. In most cases, the simpler the composition, the greater the visual impact the photograph will have.

Guidelines to good composition are just that; guidelines. You should, however, know what they are and how to apply them. Once they are second nature to you, then you may want to think about new ways to create pleasing photographs.

Center of Interest

All photographs should have a strong center of interest. Without this, the viewer's eye is left to wander aimlessly through the photograph. The center of interest should dominate the photograph, but this does not necessarily mean it has to be the largest object. Colour and positioning will also draw the eye to the center of interest.

Generally, the placement of the center of interest should correspond to the rule of thirds. Imagine that your camera's viewfinder is divided, by lines, into thirds; both vertically and horizontally. Place the center of interest near one of the four intersecting points to create a pleasing photograph. Static and unimaginative photographs result when the center of interest is placed in the exact center.

The photograph on the far left has allowed space for the peregrine falcon to look into and makes it a more successful photograph than the one on this page.

These two photographs both have a strong center of interest. Even though the Siberian tiger is not as large as the Chinese leopard, its colour and positioning catch the eye just as effectively.

Interaction between two subjects will make your photographs more interesting.

In the majority of zoo photographs, it is the animal or group of animals that create the center of interest. Having your subject(s) involved in some kind of activity makes for a more interesting and appealing photograph. With animals, look for activities such as grooming, stretching, feeding, playing, yawning or behavioral traits such as submissive or dominant poses and territorial threat displays. Researching animal

Simplifying the composition can help to increase a photograph's impact. This close-up of a patas monkey's threat display is much more effective than if I had included the rest of his body.

behavior will enable you to anticipate some of these activities or at least identify them once they happen. Your increased knowledge of the animal world will greatly help to improve your photographic results.

Camera Angle

We tend to view the world around us from our own eye level. However, this is not always the best angle from which to photograph and is a condition suffered by most novice photographers. The angle from which you take a photograph can affect the overall feeling. Observe an animal from different angles. Usually the most pleasing one is found at your subject's eye level. Some enclosures are built so that the viewer stands higher than the animals. While this factor helps to eliminate distracting backgrounds and bars, the higher camera angle affects your photograph. The subject may appear smaller and less impressive. Animals such as tigers who project an aura of power and distinction, should not be photographed from such a vantage point when you are trying to portray these characteristics. If you find yourself photographing an animal from a high angle, ensure that it is not directly under you. If you wait for the animal to move farther away, you will reduce the angle at which you are photographing and diminish this effect. The opposite holds true for small, shy animals. The higher camera angle enables you to suggest to your viewer, the animal's size and nature. Conversely, photographing smaller animals at or near their level can produce a more intimate look at the animal. This technique does require you to photograph while in some awkward positions such as lying on your stomach. Remember, even if your back gets sore and there is a kink in your neck, you are seeing things in a different perspective and producing more interesting photographs than the photographer standing beside you!

We tend to forget that every photograph does not have to be taken on a horizontal format even though that is the way we usually hold our camera. Look at the overall photograph and if the composition can be improved by a vertical format, use it.

A slightly higher camera angle and positioning the burrowing owl at the bottom of the photograph has helped to indicate the small size of this bird of prey.

Space

The center of interest does not always fill your entire photograph. Therefore, you must know what to do with the space remaining around your subject because it can affect the success of the photograph. The guideline is simple. Give space for the animal to look or walk into. A photograph of an animal walking to the left or right with its head at the edge creates a conflict for the viewer who wonders where the animal is going. Leaving space in front of the animal not only gives the viewer a sense of where the animal is going, but creates a more pleasing and dynamic photograph.

Lines

A line that directs the viewer's eye to the center of interest or through the photograph is known as a leading line. They can be vertical, horizontal, diagonal, or curved, with the latter two being the most interesting. Lines can create perspective which adds the illusion of depth to your otherwise two dimensional photograph. They can also contribute to the mood of the photograph. Horizontal lines evoke a feeling of tranquility and peacefulness while vertical lines show power and excitement.

Broken into thirds horizontally by the sky, trees and ground, this photograph evokes a peaceful setting for these Masai giraffe.

The diagonal angle of the tree trunk continually draws your eye back to the face of the African lion, making it a successful leading line.

Natural Framing

Many enclosures offer you the possibility to include a natural frame on one or both sides of the photograph. The most common natural frames, found at zoos, are trees. With the right camera angle, bushes and rocks can also be used. Natural frames are a good way of adding depth to the photograph and hiding distracting backgrounds.

Catch Lights

A catch light is a reflection or spot of light in an animal's eye that adds sparkle and life to your portraits. Sunny days produce a small spot while hazy and overcast days create more of a reflection, giving the eye a look of roundness. Have patience, as the catch light may appear and disappear depending upon the direction the animal is looking.

This photograph of an American kestrel would have lacked that feeling of life without the presence of a highlight in its eye.

Distractions

Anything that could detract from the main subject should be eliminated from the photograph. We tend to miss distracting objects because once we are involved with the subject, our eyes tend to disregard extraneous material. The camera does not have this problem; it sees everything. Therefore, extra care should be taken to watch for the following distractions:

The most obvious, for the zoo photographer interested in natural looking animal photographs, is the enclosure itself. This should be your main concern and the first thing you attempt to eliminate, both in front of, and behind the animal.

When composing your photograph, be aware of objects in the background such as tree trunks, branches, fence posts or enclosure supports that may appear as if they are growing out of the animal's head. This illusion occurs when you have positioned the subject directly in front of such an object and can be very distracting in the finished photograph. If positioned far enough behind the animal, these objects may blend into the background; especially when you use maximum aperture and depth of field is at a minimum.

Colour can not only attract the eye but distract it. If you notice a strong colour that is drawing your eye away from the main subject, attempt to adjust your camera angle to remove it. At enclosures that allow viewing on both sides of the animal, keep an eye out for brightly dressed zoo visitors as they can also put a distracting spot of colour into your background. This is something you will probably notice the moment you have taken the photograph. In that case, it is simply a matter of taking another, unless of course the animal was in an absolutely fantastic pose.

Hot spots are bright spots or lines, caused by bright sunshine reflecting off foliage or metal at an unusual angle. Using a flash can also cause hot spots if there is something in front of the subject that catches too much of the light from the flash. Unfortunately, this kind of hot spot does not appear until you get your photographs back from the lab.

The hot spot caused by light reflection off the foreground leaves has ruined an otherwise interesting photograph of a long-eared owl.

Look for objects on the animals that could detract from your otherwise natural looking photograph. The most noticeable include ear tags on hoofed animals such as deer, moose and elk, and leg bands on birds. Whenever possible, adjust your camera position or wait for the animal to move in order to block these markings from the camera's view. Zoo animals can be marked in other ways such as ear clipping or dye marking but these are not as obvious or distracting.

As a final check, look carefully along the edge of your viewfinder to make sure you have not included a portion of fence, enclosure supports, building or bars.

Animals in Action

Photographing animals in action requires a quick reaction when you see the unexpected and the patience needed to wait for the expected. Waiting is something you may find yourself doing a lot of, especially on those days when the majority of the animals are just resting or sleeping. I know this can be frustrating, but it helps if you understand a little about the nature of animal behavior. The interesting thing is that most humans do not realize that they are on a different cycle than most animals. The majority of animals are generally either active at night (nocturnal) or active in the early morning and late afternoon (crepuscular). Whereas, zoo visitors are generally active during the day (diurnal). In fact, 85 percent of all mammals are nocturnal. This certainly helps to explain the high inactivity level frequently found at zoos.

Inactivity is how many animals control their energy consumption which in the wild can sometimes mean the difference between life and death. For example, lions may rest and sleep up to 20 hours a day, looking for food for only four hours. The most inactive animals you will find at a zoo are the reptiles. Since these animals are cold blooded (ecothermic), their body temperature is controlled by their surroundings. This feature has allowed them to take a low energy approach to survival. Reptiles can eat far less often than warm blooded (endothermic) birds and mammals who must eat frequently so their bodies can maintain a constant temperature. As an example, snakes in zoos are usually given food once a week. However, they may be able to fast for months at a time.

Your best chance of finding animals active is during early morning or late afternoon and just before feeding time. Also, zoo animals, especially predators, know their keepers and react to their presence. If you want to know something about an animal, ask the keepers. If they are not busy, they are usually more than willing to talk to you. The keepers will be able to tell you when their animals are more likely to be active, when they are fed and maybe some facts about the animals as individuals.

When the situation presents itself, there are two approaches to photographing action; one is to freeze it and the other is to imply it. Freezing action is simply a matter of using a high enough shutter speed to stop the movement. When the direction of the action is coming towards the camera, you will not require as high a shutter speed as when the action is parallel to the camera. If an animal is walking quickly towards the camera, try using 1/60 of a second or higher; 1/125 of a second or higher if it is walking diagonally towards or way from

Anticipating action is essential to produce a photograph like the one on the left. After watching a couple of killer whale shows, I was able to preset my camera where I knew the animal would perform a dolphin leap. A shutter speed of 1/250 of a second froze the killer whale and the water. Backlighting made the leap much more dramatic.

A shutter speed of 1/125 of a second was enough to freeze the flamingo and the splashing water while it was bathing.

the camera and 1/250 of a second or higher if the animal is traveling parallel to the camera. This is only a guide, there are many factors such as the focal length of the lens, the speed of the lens and the distance between the animal and the camera that can affect these shutter speeds.

When photographing through an enclosure it is easiest to freeze action rather than attempting to imply it. This is due to the fact that, in order to increase the shutter speed you must open up your lens towards maximum aperture. To eliminate the bars of an enclosure you should be photographing at maximum aperture anyway. Therefore, your camera will already be set at the fastest shutter speed possible for the lighting conditions.

Implying action can be accomplished two ways. One method is to photograph at slow shutter speeds, causing the animal to be blurred against the background. This is the least effective method because generally, no part of the photograph will be in focus and every photograph should have a point which is reasonably sharp on which the eye can focus. In doing so, you hold the interest of the viewer. Sometimes, when two animals are being photographed, one animal may be out of focus because it was moving while the other animal is in focus because it was motionless. This technique works well in this case and makes for a very dramatic photograph.

A second way to imply motion is called panning. It requires you to use a slow shutter speed and follow the animal with your camera while making the exposure. In this way, you retain a relatively sharp image of the animal while blurring the background into horizontal streaks. This technique takes some practice (and film) because you must pan at the same speed as the animal is traveling. Otherwise, too much of the subject

Following this gray (timber) wolf during an exposure of 1/8 of a second has kept the wolf relatively in focus and streaked the background to imply movement. A tripod was not used in this instance.

will be blurred. The slower the shutter speed, the more difficult it becomes to follow the animal and keep it in focus, but you will create a greater illusion of speed. When you first try panning, use shutter speeds in the 1/60 or 1/30 of a second range. For an exaggerated effect, use 1/8 or 1/4 of a second.

When panning, it is best to first select a point, usually directly in front of you, where you want to take the photograph. Predators, being territorial, make this easy because you will usually find paths worn into the heavily traveled areas of their enclosures. Pick a path and pre-focus your lens on the edge of the path closest to you, and do not re-adjust your focus. When you see an animal heading down the path, start following it with your camera and the moment the animal is at the pre-focused spot, take the photograph. Remember to continue following the animal after the exposure to create a smooth motion. Whether or not you use a tripod when panning is up to you. You are looking for a feeling — not a razor sharp image.

Peak Action

Occasionally, weather conditions do not provide sufficient light to allow you to use the higher shutter speeds needed to freeze action. When you do not want to use higher speed films, there is one solution; photograph during peak action. This is the moment in every action when motion briefly stops. When an African crane jumps into the air, there is a point at the height of the jump when the bird is motionless. Anticipating this moment is the hard part. To allow for reaction time, you must actually take the photograph just before peak action occurs. If you see it in the viewfinder, you missed it on the film.

Indoor
Photography

While the majority of zoo photographs are taken outdoors under natural light, there will probably be times when you will want to photograph an animal indoors. Once indoors, there are many options open to you. The option you choose will depend on such factors as lighting conditions, the animal being photographed, and your equipment. Close-up equipment will prove useful because indoor enclosures are usually smaller, allowing you to get closer to the animals.

When a glass barrier is placed between you and the animal, remember to place your lens hood against the glass to remove any reflections or glare. I see so many people standing back from the glass when taking photographs. Reflections are even worse if you are using your flash. If you have ever photographed people standing in front of a mirror then you know what can happen. The flash burst will also ruin your attempt at photographing through glass.

When an enclosure is lit only by skylights, you will have the opportunity to photograph just as if you were outside. However, skylights can diffuse and reduce the intensity of the light, forcing you to use slow shutter speeds. This should not pose a problem, providing you are using a tripod, the animal you are photographing is not overly active, or if you are using a high speed film. The results can be very pleasing and it can be difficult to tell those photographs apart from the ones taken outdoors.

Once artificial lighting is introduced into an enclosure, you must make certain decisions because of a definite colour shift which your daylight colour film will detect but your eyes do not. Fluorescent lighting, commonly used for indoor enclosures, will cause a photograph to have an overall greenish cast if daylight colour film is used. You will also find that zoos use tungsten lighting which causes a yellowish-red cast. You must decide whether or not a colour shift will bother you. The warming effect of yellowish-red tungsten light is generally more acceptable and pleasing to the eye than the greenish cast of fluorescent lights. If you want to eliminate the effects of artificial lighting on daylight colour film then you must use either colour correction filters or a flash.

Filters

Consider a colour correction filter as an alternative to a flash when an animal is not active. Using available artificial light with a colour correction filter will produce very slow shutter speeds which may not allow you to stop even the slightest movement. Reptiles are ideal subjects for using filters because of their

Overexposing this bounce photograph of a common marmoset by three f/stops was needed to compensate for the glass and ceiling which acted as diffusers. Also, exposure was calculated based on the distance the flash had to travel which was 1.8 metres (six feet) and not the camera to subject distance which was only 0.30 metres (one foot).

inactivity. Artificial lighting also produces a more evenly lit photograph as compared to the light and dark contrasts that can result from flash illumination.

This brown pelican was photographed indoors at f/5.6 and 1/8 of a second. The only light was through a skylight.

Flash

A flash produces light similar in colour balance to that of the sun, enabling you to use regular daylight colour film when photographing indoors. A flash gives you two advantages over filters: It gives you speed (up to 1/250 of a second depending on your camera) and it gives you depth of field, especially on manual. A tripod may prove cumbersome when photographing active animals indoors while using your flash. Judge each situation accordingly and as always, if a tripod can be used, it is a good idea to use it.

Direct Flash

Direct flash results when the flash unit is placed on the hotshoe of your camera and pointed directly at the subject. The resulting illumination is similar to frontlighting. Harsh shadows will be cast behind the animal. Although, you may use a 50mm lens, the best results will be obtained with the use of a medium or longer length lens. This lens size allows you to fill more of the frame with the animal and eliminate much of the background where distracting shadows occur.

When the animal is stationary, you can take your flash off the hotshoe (if you have a sync. cord) and hold it off to the side. This will create a sidelighting effect and make a pleasing flash photograph. If you are quite close to the animal and would like to soften the light from the direct flash, simply tape a piece of facial tissue over the flash head and open your lens one or two f/stops.

Using your flash on manual when photographing through glass will yield more consistent results than when the flash is set on automatic. On manual, the flash fires at full power and is not regulated by the light sensor. Whereas, on automatic, the light sensor controls the power output of the flash. A glass barrier will reflect light at the sensor when the flash is fired and this could cause the sensor to cut the flash off too soon producing an underexposed photograph. This problem can sometimes be corrected by placing the flash head against the glass. A program camera with a program flash does not have this problem because the flash reads the light that reaches the film, not the light that reaches the light sensor of the flash and thus produces the most accurate flash exposure.

The glass of an enclosure also acts as a diffuser and reduces the amount of light that reaches the subject. On automatic, your flash sensor will adjust for this but if your flash is on manual, you will have to overexpose by opening up your lens two f/stops.

When using your flash on manual, you will gain a couple of f/stops giving you a little extra depth of field because each time you will be setting the aperture for your distance. On automatic you are given two distances between which you can move without adjusting the aperture. The flash must be set at

When using direct flash, move in on your subject to reduce the background area where harsh shadows can occur. This photograph of a white-handed gibbon was also overexposed by two f/stops to compensate for the glass.

In this photograph of a vine snake, the flash was held off to the right. This is effective with small enclosures to eliminate distracting backgrounds.

the maximum f/stop for the farthest distance in the range in order for the light sensor to adjust to all the distances.

Bounce Flash

Many flash units are equipped with a tilt head that allows you to bounce light off an object such as the ceiling of an enclosure. Light from above will eliminate the harsh shadows of direct flash and create a more evenly lit scene. If the ceiling colour is not white however, your photographs will take on the tint of the ceiling colour. Each enclosure is different so you will need to experiment to discover to what degree your photographs are affected. Whether or not you will be able to use the bounce feature on your flash for indoor zoo photography depends upon many factors: The power of your flash, the distance the light must travel, the maximum aperture of your lens, whether there is a glass barrier present and the speed of film you are using. Flashes vary in power output. The more expensive flashes are usually the more powerful ones. Since you must calculate the distance the light travels and not the distance between the camera and subject, your flash may lack the needed power. Also, the farther the light must travel, the wider the aperture you need. Your lens may not open up as wide as the flash recommends. As I have said, the glass acts as a diffuser, but now, so will the ceiling. When using a flash on manual, you will have to open up your lens at least three or four f/stops to compensate for both. On automatic your flash will normally compensate, if the flash to subject distance is not too great. Using a high speed film will make up for some of the light loss but picture quality will suffer.

Experimentation is the only answer when using bounce flash. To be on the safe side and to ensure you get good photographs, I would suggest that you use direct flash first and then try bounce flash after.

Other Flash Applications

A flash may also be used outside but only at an enclosure without bars or where you can position your camera against an enclosure. With a small flash, you can create an artificial catch light when one is not naturally present. Do not make any adjustments for the flash. Simply set the flash on the camera's hotshoe and set the flash on manual. The flash will throw enough light to place a catch light in the animal's eye, but not enough to affect exposure. If this technique is used at an enclosure where you are away from the bars, the flash will light up the bars and they will appear in your photograph.

Another application of a flash is to use it as a fill flash in plant photography. This technique can be used both indoors or out. When using your flash as a fill flash, do not set your camera to the flash sync. speed. Let the camera's light meter set the exposure. As long as the shutter speed is slower than the flash sync. speed, there will not be a problem. To calculate the distance between the flash and the subject, take the guide number of the flash and divide it by the lens aperture you are using. The figure you obtain is the distance in feet that your flash should be from the subject. To calculate the guide number of your flash, simply set the flash to match the speed of film you are using, look at the f/stop opposite 10 feet and multiply that number by 10. Let us say your flash guide number is 96 and you want to use f/16 as the aperture. Divide 96 by 16; the distance between the flash and your subject would be 6 feet. You will probably notice that the fill flash distance increases as the f/stops decrease. Therefore, maximum depth of field makes fill flash more manageable by keeping the flash distance within arm's reach. Using minimum depth of field creates longer fill flash distances that may prove awkward. In cases such as these, use a white card or tin foil to bounce the light and simulate the actual fill flash distance.

Nocturnal
Photography

Animals have certain structural adaptations to enable them to live in the world of darkness: Eyes shaped like bells to accommodate extra light sensitive cells, black and white vision, a tapetum (mirror) behind the retina to reflect unabsorbed light back into the eye so that it might be absorbed the next time, large ears and a sensitivity to high pitched sounds.

Zoos have made it possible for us to observe these creatures of the night during their most active time by reversing the day/night cycle. The light used in nocturnal enclosures is usually red in colour and permits us to view the animals without affecting their behaviour because the eyes of most nocturnal animals do not perceive red. Therefore, to them, it is still dark. Blue lights can also be used to create a moonlight effect. Under these low light conditions, using a flash makes the most sense. It will provide you with the speed required to stop any action plus the illumination needed to expose the animal. Follow the rules that apply to normal indoor flash photography.

Nocturnal photography does however present the zoo photographer with a new problem. How to accurately focus under such low light conditions. The solution is to use a small pocket flashlight. So that you do not have to hold the flashlight in one of your hands, tape it loosely to the side of your flash unit. In this way you can tilt the flashlight to point the beam of light at your subject making focusing much easier.

Not everyone's favourite animal, but the Indian fruit bat along with many other interesting nocturnal animals can provide fascinating subject matter.

By taping a small pocket flashlight to the side of my flash I was able to focus easily in the subdued light of this tawny frogmouth's enclosure.

Young Animals

Young animals are magical! I know of nothing else that can lift a person's spirits better or faster than a young animal. A visit to the zoo is always made special when we see young animals. But, for the zoo photographer, the real treat comes in photographing them.

Most people can distinguish between a young animal and an adult animal. There is no mistaking that cute baby face of a young tiger, bear or wolf. But, what of the many less familiar species you will have the opportunity to photograph at zoos. The features of these young animals may be less obvious and even more so if your photograph contains just one animal.

What the zoo photographer should try to do is make the young animal as obvious as possible. The best way to do this is to include the animal's mother or another adult in the photograph. This is not only a good way to add extra appeal to your photograph but it also creates a basis for comparison. The difference in size, body structure, and colouration can show the development that will take place as the young animal matures.

Two things to keep in mind when photographing young animals: One, do not become so involved with the subject that you forget your compositional skills or miss a certain object that could later detract from the overall photograph and two, remember, especially with smaller young animals, the most pleasing photographs are made at the animal's eye level, not your eye level.

After taking several photographs, this white rhinocerous' calf finally emerged from behind her enough to show the most prominent structural difference between them; the horn size.

The unmistakable face of a six month old Siberian tiger cub was photographed on my hands and knees in order to produce an eye level view of the subject.

Underwater
Photography

Possibly a more appropriate title would have been "Animals Underwater", just to remove any thoughts of donning mask and snorkel. From small tanks to huge pools holding millions of litres of water, aquariums and zoos provide you with many chances to photograph marine wildlife while staying perfectly dry.

You can take photographs just as if your subjects were not underwater. Even though light rays underwater will make objects appear closer, your 35mm SLR camera will still focus easily and accurately.

Underwater Viewing Windows

For large outdoor pools, underwater viewing windows are very popular and provide an interesting view of aquatic animals. Observe your viewfinder carefully and make sure that your lens hood is touching the glass in order to ensure all reflections have been removed. A polarizing filter may help eliminate some background reflections but it cannot remove a strong reflection from a point source of light. Photographing through a shaded part of the glass will help to eliminate this problem and increase colour saturation.

Unlike usual outdoor zoo photography, best results will be obtained around noon on a sunny day. Water diffuses light rays, therefore, it is better to photograph when the sun is best able to penetrate the water. In northern latitudes, this will occur in the summer months. Direct, overhead sunlight will also light a large pool more evenly. It is this intense, direct light that gives life to your underwater photographs. You will probably notice an overall colour shift depending on the pool walls. The colour shift is generally not so distracting as to detract from your photograph. Even though photographs of animals in these pools will not have a natural appearance, a small object such as a drain, can still detract from what might have been a pleasing photograph.

Normal and shorter focal length lenses (50-135mm) have the advantage of a larger maximum aperture allowing you to

This photograph of a beluga whale was taken through a viewing window with a 50mm lens. Unfortunately, the black object in the upper left corner is enough of a distraction to ruin the photograph.

By removing my flash from the hotshoe and holding it above the subject I was able to highlight the beautiful and delicate looking tentacles of this plumose sea anemone. The subject was approximately 7.6 centimetres (three inches) from the glass and a macro lens was used.

photograph at higher shutter speeds. Longer lenses may be too slow to stop any motion. Even your normal lens will probably be wide open.

Indoor Aquariums

Once you move indoors, you are again faced with artificial lighting. For slower moving fish and invertebrates, you may decide to use only the available light and possibly a colour correction filter. A tripod is essential because your shutter speeds will be very slow even with a faster lens.

A flash will provide you with more natural looking colours and the speed needed to freeze most action. Approach underwater flash photography the same as you would flash photography through glass. The only difference is that the water will act as a diffuser. Therefore, when your flash is on manual, open up three f/stops from the recommended aperture, to compensate for both the glass and the water. Whenever you have a free hand, remove the flash from the hotshoe and hold it off to the side for a more pleasing type of lighting.

The photograph on the left was taken using only the aquarium's tungsten lights. The photograph below was taken using direct flash held off to the left side. Although the flash has rendered the colours of this speckled eel more accurately, tungsten light still produced an acceptable photograph.

When photographing at smaller aquariums or slow moving animals use a tripod if possible. Simply set up and wait for the animal to swim or move in front of the lens. A tripod with independently working legs will prove invaluable in this situation. It ensures your lens hood is touching or as close as possible to the glass.

The lens you use indoors depends on the size of the animal and the size of the tank or aquarium. Have a macro lens, close-up equipment, and even a wide angle lens ready as they will all prove to be useful in various situations.

Anticipating the direction of this Pacific prawn's movement, I set up my equipment and waited for it to move into the photograph.

Due to the size of this lemon shark's enclosure, my flash was only able to light the shark itself, plunging the background into total darkness. The shark was photographed with a 50mm lens.

Plants

On those days when the animals seem to have conspired against you or thoughts of a fur coat enter your mind while you are photographing wolves on a cold winter day, maybe it is time to take a break from the animals and take advantage of one of the other photographic opportunities that a zoo offers.

Many zoos display a wide variety of exotic, tropical and native plants. The shapes and colours in the plant world are even more vast than those of the animal kingdom. When surrounded by such beauty, it is easy to see things superficially. Do not fall into the habit of photographing a plant or its flower the first way you see it. Walk around the subject and view it from as many different angles as possible. Remember, with any photograph you take, you should decide what has drawn you to that particular subject and emphasize that element. This is the only way to avoid disappointment when photographing plants and flowers.

Close-ups

Although striking photographs can be achieved in nature showing the plant in its environment, at a zoo, we are dealing mainly with close-up photography. The tools include close-up rings, extension tubes, macro or macro zoom lenses and, without any question, a tripod and cable release. This equipment enables you to explore the intricate patterns, delicate shapes and interesting textures of the plant world.

Hazy and overcast days emphasize the delicate and fragile nature of some plants and their flowers while also

Close-up equipment allows you to explore the beauty of the plant world. The flower of this rhododendren was photographed using a macro zoom lens at a reproduction ratio of 1:4.

The translucent quality of this petticoat palm was emphasized by the use of backlighting.

Taking advantage of minimum depth of field and selective focusing (especially in macro photography), has isolated a small group of lily-flowered tulips and surrounded them with a beautiful impressionistic image.

producing the most accurate colours. Use sidelighting to emphasize shape and backlighting to enhance the translucent quality of a plant.

The major factor affecting close-up photography is depth of field. You know the closer you are to your subject the less depth of field there is, well, in close-up photography the depth of field can be measured in millimetres! This necessitates careful camera positioning. Make sure that the front of your lens is parallel to the part of the plant you want to be sharp.

Minimum aperture works best when you want to document a plant and need maximum depth of field to ensure as much of your subject is in focus as possible. However, minimum depth of field, when used effectively, can isolate a solitary leaf, petal or stamen and surround it with impressionistic colours and shapes. The photographic results you can achieve are exquisite. Using minimum depth of of field is my favourite technique for photographing plants because it allows me to be more creative.

Calculating Long Exposures

When you are photographing plants indoors or on overcast days, you will be working with long exposures if you want to obtain maximum depth of field. It is important to remember that your camera's light meter is only a guide. Just because the shutter speeds only go to one second, does not mean you cannot use longer exposures if light levels and depth of field requirements demand them.

Let us say you have set up a photograph you would like to take and have decided you want maximum depth of field.

A look at button mums from a different viewpoint has added creativity and appeal to this photograph.

You set your aperture to f/22 and notice that the light meter is not giving you a reading. To get a reading, simply start opening up your lens and at f/5.6 for example you get a reading of one second. It now becomes a matter of mathematics. From f/5.6 you go f/8, 11, 16, 22. Moving in this direction, you are cutting the amount of light that reaches the film in half for a total of four times. To produce an equivalent exposure, you must now double the shutter speed four times. One second then becomes 2, 4, 8, 16 seconds. Now, instead of f/5.6 at one second you have f/22 at 16 seconds. But, this is still not an accurate exposure because reciprocity failure (page 31) has not been taken into account. The exposure you will actually use is f/22 at 24 seconds. You then set your lens to f/22, the shutter speed dial to "B" and use a cable release to hold the shutter open for 24 seconds.

Plants do not always remain motionless for long exposures and any movement will affect sharpness. Photographing on calm days or setting up a wind block (which can double as a reflector) will help to alleviate this problem.

Reflectors

A reflector made of aluminum foil or white paper can effectively lighten a shaded area to bring back some of the detail that is normally lost. Place the reflector under or beside the area you want to lighten. When using foil, crumple it first then stretch it back into its original shape. Jiggle the reflector during the exposure, to produce an even distribution of light.

People

If you enjoy photographing people, a zoo will certainly provide you with plenty of subject material. There will be numerous opportunities involving people with everything from animals to ice cream. For this reason, zoos lend themselves well to candid photography. Posed situations created when people or children do what you want them to do can introduce an element of tension which will show in the finished photograph. This type of staged photograph records an event, but a good candid photograph tells a story.

Candid Photography

Candid photography does not necessarily mean you have to sneak around or hide behind every tree and fence. It is simply a matter of not being obvious. People may see you walking around with your camera, but because there are so many people walking around with cameras, they will soon forget about you.

Good candid photographs not only require an ability to observe and anticipate but also, making sure your equipment is ready when you are. Of course, good old plain luck is pretty important too! A few simple steps will ensure your camera is ready when you are. Your camera should be carried at your side (yes, you can forget about your tripod) with the exposure preset and the focusing ring of your lens set at infinity. When you see a potentially good situation, bring your camera up to your eye, focus (you should only have to focus once), depress the shutter at the right moment and return the camera to your side. Setting the exposure beforehand means you must predetermine the aperture and shutter speed for the lighting conditions. The easiest way to do this is to take a meter reading off your hand. The light falling on your hand, will be the same light falling on your subject. If you have an automatic or program camera, you have the option of letting the camera control the exposure for you. In this case, the camera will also adjust for any quick change in lighting conditions.

Using faster shutter speeds allows you to freeze an action or reaction by your subject and also control camera shake from hand holding. Favouring faster shutter speeds, means you will lose depth of field. Therefore, your focusing must not only be quick, it must be accurate. To achieve this, set your lens on infinity after each photograph. When you bring your camera up to your eye, you will only be able to turn the focusing barrel one way; the right way! As soon as the viewfinder appears sharp, take the photograph. Do not get into the habit of going a little past just to make sure you really were in focus. You will than have to place your subject into focus again.

Sometimes the best way to photograph the fun a child is having is for you to also experience it.

Candid photography is easier if you minimize the amount of equipment you use. I have already mentioned that a tripod is not necessary in this instance and if you rely on available light, you can also eliminate your flash.

Lenses in the 85 to 135mm range are good for people photography. They allow you to stand farther away from the subject and they can be easily hand held. A zoom lens is ideal for candid photography because you can zoom in and out, depending on the situation and the number of people involved.

To take good candid photographs, you must frequent the areas where good candids happen. Look to childrens' zoos or petting areas for excellent opportunities in close-up interaction between people and animals. Stand where ice cream is sold (preferably in the summer) and see if you do not find some interesting photographs. Also, playground areas for children are a spot for action photographs.

Children

The thing to remember about children is they are less predictable, have shorter attention spans and higher energy levels than most adults. This makes photographing them an adventure, to say the least, especially if they are your own. The zoo is a place where children can learn and have fun at the same time. Let them go where they want and do what they like (to a point of course). You should just follow them and take advantage of whatever happens. There are so many things to attract a child's attention and curiousity at a zoo that sometimes, the animals are what a child is least interested in. It always makes me smile when I see parents desperately

This photograph of a girl about to get incredibly wet was the result of patience, timing and a lot of film. A shutter speed of 1/125 of a second has implied a feeling of motion by not totally freezing the water.

trying to get their child to look at a certain animal when he or she has focused his or her attention on something else. It could be another animal (usually one of much less grandeur), another child, or even better, another child with food. As a photographer (and parent), you must take it all in stride, but most of all, have fun. If you get frustrated, annoyed or angry, your photographs will certainly suffer. By practicing technique and timing and exercising patience, you will begin to produce candid photographs that are full of life and tell a story.

The subject's face does not always have to be visible to make a photograph successful. By standing behind the boy in this example, we become a part of the photograph and share his interest as he watches a domestic goose.

Equipment Check List

Besides the basic equipment, camera body, lenses, flash and tripod, your gadget bag should contain a few extras. Even though I mentioned planning what you want to photograph ahead of time, it does not hurt to be prepared for any opportunity. Therefore, it is a good idea to have all of the following items in your gadget bag (You will have to carry all of this gear so have a comfortable bag with a nice wide strap):

Film

It seems funny to mention, but I have seen too many people get caught without extra film. To be on the safe side, carry at least two rolls of 36 exposure film for a half day of photography.

Batteries

Carry extra batteries for your camera, flash, motor drive, and anything else that uses them. Today's automatic and program cameras will not function at all without batteries.

Lens Cleaning Equipment

Include lens cleaning tissue, fluid, and compressed air or a blower brush as part of your lens cleaning kit. Do not use anything but lens cleaning tissue to wipe your lens. Never put lens cleaning fluid directly on your lens; place one or two drops on a crumpled piece of lens tissue first and use it to wipe the lens. Use care when cleaning a lens with compressed air, the can must be upright or the gas inside could escape as a liquid. Short blasts of air are better than long ones. Do not hold the release nozzle too close to your lens to ensure that the cold compressed air does not damage the multi-coating on the front element.

Filters

Include an ultraviolet or skylight filter for protecting your lenses, a polarizing filter to reduce reflections and increase colour saturation, a magenta (FLD) filter and a blue (80A) filter to correct for fluorescent and tungsten lighting respectively when using daylight colour film.

Lens Hoods

You should have one for every lens you own.

Shade Maker

Make the one shown below or use a black cloth held in place by clothes pins. This will improve the colour saturation of your photographs when positioned against the bars of an enclosure.

White Paper or Tinfoil

Helpful in plant photography as a reflector and also to attract an animal's attention.

Small Flashlight

For when the urge to go nocturnal strikes.

Plastic Bag

To protect your camera while photographing in bad weather.

Note Pad

Finally, a note pad and pen so you can write any special information such as the name of the animal or an exposure setting.

Construction of shade maker

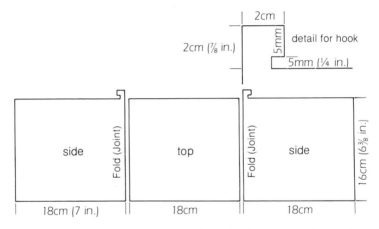

Cut three pieces of single weight black illustration board to the sizes and shapes indicated. Lay flat and tape the joints with black masking tape, flip over and tape other side. Fold sides down (black side in) and hook onto the mesh. Place lens inside.

Care and Presentation

High temperatures, humidity, light and gases from solvents, cleaners, and mothballs all shorten the life of photographic materials by causing the dyes to prematurely fade. Therefore, care should be taken to properly store your negatives, prints and slides. Normal storage conditions should include a dark box, closet or room with temperatures under 21C (70F) and a low humidity level (15 to 40 percent). Even under these conditions some films will fade earlier than others. If you want to enjoy your photographs for at least your lifetime; black and white film or Kodachrome film are what you should be using. Under normal conditions, black and white negatives can last one hundred years or more. Kodachrome will usually not show significant dye fading for at least 50 years. With other types of slide films, fading can start between 10 and 20 years. Colour negatives have the shortest lift span and fading can occur after only 2 to 5 years. Optimum storage under refrigeration can extend any of these times considerably.

Storing unexposed film in the refrigerator or freezer is not necessary but can delay the film's expiration date. Be sure to store the film in its original box. When it is removed from the refrigerator for use, allow a warm up time of 1 to 3 hours or 3 to 5 hours if the film was in the freezer.

Care of Slides and Negatives

You will have put a great deal of time and effort into your zoo photographs and therefore they should be treated with care. Hold slides by their mounts and negatives by their edges. Never touch the image area with your fingers. Finger prints, especially on the emulsion side will be next to impossible to remove. If you frequently handle your slides or negatives, individual clear plastic sleeves can be purchased. You can also buy sheets which will hold 20 slides or 36 exposures of negatives. Be sure to purchase acid-free photographic sheets, otherwise the acid in certain plastics over a period of time, can draw the colour from your negatives or slides and ruin them.

Organization

Before you place your negatives, prints or slides in storage, they must first be organized. If you use slides, your zoo photographs can be divided into the groups of animals (e.g. cats) and then broken down into species or individual animals (e.g. leopards). Write the name of the animal and the zoo on the slide mount so it can be easily identified. Writing the animal's name in a notebook at the time you photographed it will make this task much easier. Slides can be stored in many ways including the original boxes from the processing lab, projector trays, clear plastic sheets or file boxes made of metal or plastic.

Organizing negatives can be done using plastic storage sheets which are three-hole punched. Code your negatives and the back of your prints for easy reference, in the event you want a reprint or enlargement. A typical code at the top of a negative sheet might be 85-6; meaning the sixth roll of film you have taken in 1985. The corresponding prints would then be numbered 85-6-1, 85-6-2 and so on to match the negative numbers. The most practical way to store prints for viewing is in albums, preferably under plastic to protect them from finger prints. No matter how you organize your photographs, you should be consistent and it should be done everytime you get your film back from processing.

Showing Your Work

Once your zoo photograph collection begins to increase, be very critical of your work. Your collection is only as good as your worst photograph; a print or slide thrown out today, may have been your best a year ago. You cannot keep everything (although, many people do). If you would not show somebody one of your bad photographs, why keep it?

When putting together a slide show be selective and only show a few of each animal depicting a variety of activities. Once you have a large collection, you can also make your shows more specific in content. Birds of prey, primates or cats are some examples. Inform your audience about the animals and what they are doing.

When presenting your slides, do not leave a slide on the screen for very long unless you are talking about that animal. The visual impact of your slide will occur instantly. The longest a slide should be shown is 10 seconds. Remember, less is better, keep your slide show moving.

Showing people your photographs, if you have prints, can best be done with an album. However, you will find it difficult to show your prints to more than one or two people at once.

The photographs you take are mainly for your enjoyment so have enlargements made from your favourite slides or prints and display them together on a wall. Put up new ones when you feel like a change and perhaps give the old ones away. A photograph of someone's favourite animal, taken by you, can make a very special gift.

Extinction, Endangered animals and Zoos

More than ever before, we should be aware of the threat of extinction that many animals face today. Since the industrial revolution, man has drastically altered the environment to suit his own needs with little thought given to the animals who also share this planet. It is this thoughtlessness, that has caused hundreds of animals to disappear forever while others teeter on the brink of extinction.

Nature is fragile and delicate. It is made up of inter-dependencies which create a balance. Every animal has a specific niche in this balance. When the balance of nature is upset by man, an animal must do something that can be extremely difficult, and that is to try to adjust to an altered environment. The reason for the difficulty lies in the fact that every species possesses a special set of fine-tuned features that enables it to survive in a specific habitat. These features may lack effectiveness when the animal is faced with a changed environment or food source. Man is unique. When he is confronted with a new environment, he has the ability to change it to suit his needs.

Natural control of wildlife populations occurs through predation, disease, accidental deaths and a shortage of food and water. Man has tampered with this natural control through the introduction of fire, weapons, agriculture and pollution. When an animal becomes extinct due to a tampering with nature, there are two things that can happen. First, several other animals may unexpectedly become endangered or extinct because of the interdependencies of animals. Or secondly, another species may become too numerous, placing a strain on the food chain. In either case, we are reaching a point in time where this balance must be stabilized or we risk the demise of life on this planet as we know it.

Extinction is a natural process that man has accelerated. Before man appeared on this planet, extinction of a species usually occured every thousand years. Man has altered this rate to the extent that at present, more than one animal or plant species becomes extinct every day. If current trends continue, it could be one species every hour! Extinction is not a problem faced only by other countries. Canada and the United States are prime contributors in the extermination and endangering of wildlife. An animal is usually placed on the endangered species list when its total world wide population drops below two thousand. This number can fluctuate because of the many factors considered when deciding if an animal is endangered, such as: The size and condition of the animal's habitat, the animal's reproduction rate and the amount of competition between species found in that habitat.

Even the national bird of the United States has not been spared from man's misuse of the environment. Pesticides are the bald eagle's greatest enemy and have seriously affected their ability to reproduce.

When visiting zoos look for their symbol to identify a vanishing animal. The symbol will indicate an animal species that is threatened with extinction; an animal whose survival and reproduction are in immediate peril.

Several North American animals threatened with extinction when this book was printed include the wood bison, eastern cougar, gray wolf (U.S. only), swift fox (Canada only), black-footed ferret (considered to be the rarest mammal in North America), sea otter, bald eagle (U.S. only), California condor, peregrine falcon, blue whale, Atlantic white fish, timber rattlesnake and the American crocodile. These are just a few animals from a very long list of approximately 200 animals.

Probably no other animal has been so wrongly persecuted by man as the wolf. In the United States, the gray (timber) wolf has been hunted to near extinction and now occupies only one percent of its original range.

Habitat destruction is the number one reason for animals becoming endangered or extinct (secondary reasons include extensive hunting and poaching, pesticides and poisoning). As our human population continues to increase, our demand for residential, agricultural and industrial space grows. This places a tremendous strain on the animal population which cannot compete with the onslaught by the ultimate of mammals.

Only in this last century has a serious interest in conservation developed. Perhaps it comes from the realization that animals are disappearing at a more accelerated rate than ever before. Through the work of concerned conservationists, research scientists and zoos, we are now trying to save what could so easily be lost. One important short term factor today lies in the setting aside of land for parks and reserves to ensure the preservation of as many species as possible. More importantly though, on the long term scale, is the education of the world's population to the wise use of the earth's natural resources and the reduction in the rate of population growth.

Zoos

To most people, the zoo is simply a pleasant place to spend an afternoon. Today's zoos, however, have become the last refuge for many endangered animals. Cases exist where an animal may be extinct in the wild but still found in zoos or where the captive population of a species outnumbers its counterparts in the wild. Zoos also play an important role in informing the public about wildlife conservation. I am certain that without the help of zoos, there would be many more people unaware of the plight of today's wildlife.

Zoos are actively involved in the captive breeding of endangered animals. To increase the captive population, zoos work together by exchanging animals and information. It can be a risky and expensive proposition to transport an animal for breeding but it is also necessary if the problem of inbreeding is to be controlled. Inbreeding weakens the genetic structure of a species and can lead to abnormalities in future generations. Artificial insemination, embryo transplants and the storage of frozen unfertilized eggs and semen are now in the early stages, but may someday reduce inbreeding or possibly save a species from extinction. Building a strong captive population of an endangered species increases the possibility of releasing that animal back into a protected wild area at some future date, giving it a second chance at survival.

Most zoos, committed to the survival of the world's animals, are replacing their cages with natural habitat enclosures. Natural objects and terrain create a more pleasing atmosphere for viewing the animals. More importantly, they also place the animals at ease so that the chances of successful breeding are much higher. Natural habitat enclosures are extremely expensive. Without the support of the community and charitable organizations, a zoo may be forced to delay the rate at which it can construct new enclosures.

If you are at all interested in animals and would like to provide assistance, you can start by supporting the zoo in your area. A strong membership can greatly influence the funds a zoo receives.

For information on ways in which you can help particular animals worldwide contact:

The World Wildlife Fund Canada
Suite 201, 60 St. Clair Avenue East
Toronto, Ontario
M4T 1N5

The World Wildlife Fund
1601 Connecticut Avenue North West
Washington, D.C. 20009

About the Author

Ina Sanderman

The author, Christopher Clark, is a professional graphic designer who has been involved in photography since he was a teenager. His interest in animals and zoo photography was sparked after moving to Alberta in 1980.

Since that time, the author has photographed at zoos, aquariums and wildlife parks throughout Canada and in the United States. The knowledge gained through this experience has given him a special understanding about zoo photography.

The sensitivity shown by the author in his photographs comes from a genuine concern and love for wildlife. As a docent (volunteer) at the Calgary Zoo he was able to share these feelings with school children and adults. It was also here that he spent many enjoyable hours with some special animals.

An opening in the Calgary Zoo's graphics department provided a unique opportunity for the author to combine his talents as a designer with his desire to be close to the animals that he takes pleasure in photographing.

Always setting new challenges and goals for himself, the author decided there was a need for a book on the subject of zoo photography alone. The finished product of this effort, you now hold in your hands.